ISBN 9781549970597

D1714478

Introduction

Isaiah 53 is one of the most important chapters of all Scripture. Christians state that it speaks of Jesus as the Messiah, but Jewish scholars say it speaks of Israel as a nation. Most Jewish people have never read it.

I have always been taught that Isaiah 53 is never read in any synagogue in the world, but I have recently learned that it is apparently read in some Sephardic synagogues at Passover. It appears that the Ashkenazim wanted to remove it from their Bibles, but the Sephardim do read it, but don't understand it. In the weekly readings in Ashkenazi synagogues they end at Isaiah 52:11 one week and pick up with Is. 54:1 the next week. No one notices that this chapter is missing. So, when you show this chapter or read this chapter of Isaiah to most Jewish people they say that it is from the New Testament and that it speaks about Jesus. But Isaiah 53 was written more than 700 years before Jesus was born. There is no way that it could have ever been from the New Testament. There is no possibility that it could have been inserted by missionaries as some rabbis have claimed.

There is strong evidence (from the Jewish sources) that the Old Testament canon was completed by 450 B.C. and its Greek translation, the Septuagint, is dated about two hundred fifty years before Christ. Therefore, a complete Hebrew text from which this Greek translation would be derived must have existed **prior to the third century B.C**. It was included in the Jewish canon of Scriptures by Ezra the Scribe when he convened the council known as The Great Synagogue in 440 B.C.

As to Dead Sea (or Qumran) scrolls, archaeological studies arrived at a date ranging from the second century B.C. to the first century A.D. Paleographers studied the style of writing and arrived at dates ranging from the third century B.C. to the first century A.D. Scientists, using the radiocarbon dating method, dated the scrolls to range from the fourth century B.C. to the first century A.D. Since all the methods came to a similar conclusion, the scrolls date as early as the third century B.C. to the first century A.D.

The photo on the next page is from the website of the Israel Museum and Shrine of the Book in Jerusalem.[1] There you can find the passage in column XLIV (44). The page or column of the scroll begins with Isaiah 52:13 at the top and Isaiah 53 begins where the mark in the right margin is located.

---

[1] http://dss.collections.imj.org.il/isaiah?id=1:1

Isaiah 53 from "The Great Isaiah Scroll" of the famous "Dead Sea Scrolls"

Mathematical and Grammatical Construction

The mathematical and grammatical challenges of writing such a passage as the Messianic poem of Isaiah 40-66 are far beyond comprehension. How was it possible both from a mathematical standpoint and a grammatical view to write this poem? The message is one thing and is most discussed, but the patterns are almost never discussed or even seen by most commentators. To my own knowledge only J. Sidlow Baxter has ever noticed this before. I remember hearing him speak on this for a week in a conference in the early 1970's. He gives snippets of those studies in his great book "The Master Theme of the Bible", published by Tyndale House in 1973.

The book of Isaiah is a miniature of the Bible. There are 66 chapters in Isaiah and 66 books of the Bible. The Bible is divided into two sections, and so is Isaiah:

- The Tenach (Old Testament) consists of 39 books dealing with Jewish history

- The first part of Isaiah consists of 39 chapters of prose dealing with Jewish history

- The New Testament consists of 27 books dealing with the Messiah

- The second part of Isaiah consists of 27 chapters dealing with the Messiah

Isaiah 40-66 is a long Messianic poem divided into three sections of exactly the same length, each containing 9 chapters. Each section ends with the same phrase, but stated slightly differently. And the last verse, or third statement is an expansion of the previous two.

- Is. 48:22 reads: "There is no peace, saith the LORD, unto the wicked."

- Is. 57:21 reads: "There is no peace, saith my God, to the wicked."

- Is. 66:24 reads: "And they shall go forth and look on the carcasses of the men that have transgressed against me: for their worm shall not die, neither shall their fire be quenched; and they shall be an abhorring unto all flesh."

The center chapter of the center section is Isaiah 53. Everything before Is. 53 looks forward to that chapter and everything after Is. 53 looks back to that chapter.

The center verse of the center chapter is Is. 53:7. And the exact center of this long Messianic poem is the phrase "he is brought as a lamb to the slaughter". The exact center of the long Messianic poem and the center verse, the center phrase is the word "lamb".

The Text

The passage actually begins in Is. 52:13, but vv 13-15 are the introduction to the main topic, that of Is. 53, even though we see here a very graphic description of the crucifixion of the servant. It is the warm-up to the main event. Here we see God's servant being introduced and His manner of death described. The topic of Is. 53 is summarized in these 3 verses. Here, in these three verses we see a glimpse into the most horrific death possible of a human being. The Servant, the Messiah, the Son of God, Jehovah, the Creator of the universe, the Prince of Peace will be so hated that He will be beaten, scourged, cut, pierced and marred beyond all recognition, then nailed to a cross. No depiction by Hollywood or any artist or literary description even comes close to portraying or illustrating that scene.

In each verse we see a statement and then three sub-statements. This is a style of Hebrew poetry known as extended parallels. In this style a statement is made and then the thought is extended two, or in this case, three times. Note the following examples:

> **Isaiah 52:13**
> Behold, my servant shall deal prudently,
> * he shall be exalted,
> * and extolled,
> * and be very high.

This is a reference to the bronze serpent on the pole in Num. 21:8-9. Jesus tied these two passages together in John. 3:14 in his conversation with Nicodemus. He again referred to these passages in John 8:28 when he declared, "When ye have lifted up the Son of man, then shall ye know that I am he and that I do nothing of myself; but as my Father hath taught me, I speak these things." Then in John 12:32 Jesus said, "And I, if I be lifted up from the earth, will draw all men unto me."

Paul refers to this passage in Phil. 2:8-11, which reads, "And being found in fashion as a man, he humbled himself and became obedient unto death, even the death of the cross. Wherefore God also hath highly exalted him, and given him a name which is above every name: that at the name of Jesus every knee should bow, of things in heaven, and things in earth, and things under the earth; and that every tongue should confess that Jesus Christ is Lord, to the glory of God the Father."

> **Isaiah 52:14**
> As many as were astonished at thee;
> - his visage was so marred
> - more than any other man,
> - and his form more than the sons of men.

Cf. Is. 50:6 where we read that the Messiah's beard would be plucked out and his face would be beyond recognition.

No painting or description of the crucifixion is adequate. If one can recognize Jesus, the depiction is not detailed or graphic enough. He was so brutally marred, cut, beaten, etc. that no one could really recognize Him. They knew it was Him, but He was totally unrecognizable.

Most depictions of the crucifixion are from the New Testament. But what is there isn't nearly as graphic as what we see here.

> **Isaiah 52:15**
> So shall he sprinkle many nations;
> - the kings shall shut their mouths at him:
> - for that which and not been told them shall they see;
> - and that which they had not heard shall they consider.

This is a reference to the Levitical sacrifices. The priest offering the sacrifice and who would sprinkle the blood had to be ritually pure.

This verse is quoted by Paul in Romans 15:21 and 16:25, then again in Ephesians 3:5-9.

Jesus' crucifixion was so horrible that even kings would want to turn away from the sight. If it were to be depicted in paintings or on film today people would protest the horrible graphic details.

The style of poetry of Is. 53:1-12

The style of poetry changes at this point to what is called completive parallels. Here the second statement is the re-statement of the first, but from a different perspective. Instead of the lines rhyming as in most poetry, the thoughts are parallel. Or, in other words, the same thought is stated twice, the first time from man's perspective and the second time from God's perspective. The response can be different depending on the perspective.

Note verse 1.

Man's perspective: Who hath believed our report?

God's perspective: To whom is the arm of the LORD revealed?

This sets the theme of this chapter. Also, vv. 1-6 show the vicarious atonement of the Messiah from man's perspective. But vv. 7-12 show the vicarious atonement of the Messiah from God's perspective, thus making the second half of the chapter a completive parallel to the first half.

The seven statements of the vicarious atonement from man's perspective are:

1. v. 4: *He* hath borne **our** griefs
2. v. 4: and carried **our** sorrows
3. v. 5: *He* was wounded for **our** transgressions
4. v. 5: *He* was bruised for **our** iniquities
5. v. 5: the chastisement of **our** peace is on *him*
6. v. 5: and with *his* stripes **we** are healed
7. v. 6: the LORD hath laid on *him* the iniquity of **us** all.

The seven statements of the vicarious atonement from God's perspective are:

1. v. 8: for the transgression of **my** people was *he* stricken
2. v. 10: Thou shalt make *his* soul an offering for sin
3. v. 11: By *his* knowledge shall **my** righteous servant justify many
4. v. 11: for *he* shall bear **their** iniquities
5. v. 12: *He* was numbered with the **transgressors**
6. v. 12: and *he* bore the sin of **many**
7. v. 12: and *[he]* made intercession for the **transgressors.**

Now let us focus on the central portion of the central theme of the center section of this poem, v. 7.

V. 7, the focal point of this chapter, reads: "He was oppressed, and he was afflicted, yet he opened not his mouth: he is brought as a lamb to the slaughter, and as a sheep before her shearers is dumb, so he openeth not his mouth."

Everything in this long Messianic poem preceding this verse and everything following it points to the statement "he was brought as a lamb to the slaughter". When Jesus appeared at the location where John the Baptist was baptizing people, John looked up and cried out, "**Behold, the Lamb of God, which taketh away the sins of the world.**" (Jn. 1:29). This is a direct reference to Is. 53. That one statement summarizes the whole of Isaiah 53. Jesus is the Lamb. He is the Lamb of God. And He died for the sins of the world.

V. 7 is played out in all four gospels and in the book of Acts.

Note:

- **Matthew 26:62-63** "And the high priest arose, and said unto him, **Answerest thou nothing?** what is it which these witness against thee? But Jesus held his peace. And the high priest answered and said unto him, I adjure thee by the living God, that thou tell us whether thou be the Christ, the Son of God."

- **Mark 15:3-5** "And the chief priests accused him of many things: but he answered nothing. And Pilate asked him again, saying, **Answerest thou nothing?** behold how many things they witness against thee. But Jesus yet answered nothing; so that Pilate marveled."

- **Luke 23:8-9** "And when Herod saw Jesus, he was exceeding glad: for he was desirous to see him of a long season, because he had heard many things of him; and he hoped to have seen some miracle done by him. Then he questioned with him in many words; but **he answered him nothing**."

- **John 19:8-9** "When Pilate therefore heard that saying, he was the more afraid; And went again into the judgment hall, and saith unto Jesus, Whence art thou? But **Jesus gave him no answer**."

- **This verse is also quoted in Acts 8:32-33** "The place of the scripture which he read was this, He was led as a sheep to the slaughter; and like a lamb dumb before his shearer, **so opened he not his mouth**: In his humiliation his judgment was taken away: and who shall declare his generation? for his life is taken from the earth."

Portions of Is. 53 are quoted or referred to in the New Testament many times. In every case it speaks about Jesus and His death, burial and resurrection for our sins. Jesus paid our debt. He did more than cover our sins, He paid the price which none of us could afford. No amount of money, no number of good deeds and no appeals can atone for our sins. The only one who could do this would be someone who had lived in this world without committing even one sin. Jesus is that person. He is the Lamb of God.

Jesus paid our debt. We need only to repent and accept that payment. In Romans 3:23 we read, "All have sinned and fallen short of the glory of God." Three chapters later in Romans 6:23 we read, "The wages of sin is death, but the gift of God is eternal life." And in between those two, in Romans 5:8 & 9 we discover, "God commendeth his love toward us, in that, while we were yet sinners, Christ died for us. Much more then, being now **justified by his blood**, the blood of the lamb, we shall be saved from wrath through him."

Note the parallel between Is. 53: 6 and 8. They both look to v. 7. But in v. 6 Jesus died for **_everyone_**. In v. 8 He died specifically for the **_Jewish people_**.

Jesus, Himself, said in **John 14:6**, "I am the way, the truth, and the life; no man cometh to the father, but by me." There is no other way. You cannot work for your salvation. You cannot buy your salvation. Jesus is the ONLY way. Your debt has been paid. If you have not done so, appropriate it today. Open your heart to Jesus, the Jewish Messiah. Isaiah wrote to a Jewish audience about the Jewish Messiah. Jesus spoke to a Jewish audience. It is by God's grace that we who are not Jewish are included in this great message.

Never forget the words of v. 5, "**All we like sheep have gone astray; we have turned every one to his own way; and the LORD hath laid on him the iniquity of us all.**"

> **Isaiah 53:1**
> Who hath believed our report?
> And to whom is the arm of the LORD revealed?

The history of the world is summed up in these two questions. Every one who has ever lived and whoever will live in the future comes under one or both of these questions. Every act ever taken from Adam to the end of eternity is a reflection of these two questions. Every war that has or will be fought, every ruler that has or will rule, every soldier that has or will serve, everyone and every act or thought comes under these two questions. **_Everyone either accepts or rejects God's message._** The Lord reveals Himself to us all, but not all see or believe what they do see. _Salvation is available to everyone, but only a very few will respond and walk the narrow path in order to enter the strait gate._

The first question is from man's perspective and the second one is from God's perspective. Let us look at the first question first.

"Who hath believed our report?"

Most people not only don't believe "our report", but kill the messenger, whether he be a prophet, missionary, pastor or simply a believer trying to share the Gospel of Jesus Christ. Note what Jesus had to say about this in Matthew 7:13-14 states, "Enter ye in at the strait gate: for wide is the gate, and broad is the way, that leadeth to destruction, and many there be which go in thereat: Because strait is the gate, and narrow is the way that leadeth unto life, and few there be that find it."

Again, Jesus spoke while on the Mt. of Olives overlooking the city of Jerusalem, which is recorded in Matt. 23:29-30, "Woe unto you Scribes and Pharisees, hypocrites! because ye build the tombs of the prophets, and garnish the sepulchers of the righteous, and say, 'If we had been in the days of our fathers, we would not have been partakers with them in the blood of the prophets.' Wherefore ye be witnesses unto yourselves, that ye are the children of them which killed the prophets."

Then in Matt. 23:34-37 we read, "Wherefore, behold, I send unto you prophets, and wise men, and scribes: and some of them ye shall kill and crucify, and some of them shall ye scourge in your synagogues, and persecute them from city to city: that upon you may come all the righteous blood shed upon the earth, from the blood of righteous Abel unto the blood of Zacharias son of Barachias, whom ye slew between the temple and the altar. Verily I say unto you, 'All these things shall come upon this generation.' O Jerusalem, Jerusalem thou that killest the prophets, and stonest them which are sent unto thee, how often would I have gathered thy children together, even as a hen gathereth her chickens under her wings, and ye would not!"

In John 12:37-38 we read, "But though he had done so many miracles before them, yet they believed not on him: that the saying of Esaias the prophet might be fulfilled, which he spake, Lord, who hath believed our report? and to whom hath the arm of the Lord been revealed?"

In John 12:39-40 the passage continues with how the arm of the Lord was not revealed to them by quoting Is. 6:9-10, which reads, "Therefore they could not believe, because that Esaias said again, 'He hath blinded their eyes, and hardened their heart; that they should not see with their eyes, nor understand with their heart, and be converted, and I should heal them."

What happened throughout history to those who proclaimed the ways of the Lord? They were shunned, laughed at, scorned, falsely accused, thrown into prison, sold into slavery, killed and even crucified. History hasn't changed much. Today Christians are being shunned, laughed at, scorned, falsely accused, thrown into prison, sold into slavery, killed and even crucified. All you have to do is read the newspaper, listen to a news report or open your computer. Christians are being called intolerant, homophobes, racists and much more.

World leaders throughout history were worshipped and proclaimed as gods. This was true with the pharaohs in Egypt, the kings of Sumer, Babylon, Persia, Greece, Rome and more. Note the situation in Daniel 3 with Nebuchadnezzar's large statue and the 3 Hebrews who were thrown into the furnace because they refused to worship him. Daniel constantly battled kings on this issue. Some believed his report. But throughout history most national leaders have rejected the report, shunned God and proclaimed themselves to be gods.

Cain justified his murder of Abel, because his own sacrifice was rejected by God. After all, his sacrifice didn't involve the killing of an animal. That animal hadn't committed any sin, so why should it have to suffer? Cain's vegetarian sacrifice was better, more colorful, more nutritious, more loving and peaceful. Cain could be the patriarch of PETA (People for the Ethical Treatment of Animals). We see the same actions today. People think they can come to God through their own contrived ideas. Even many Christians want God to be their servant rather than they serving Him.

The Ten Commandments are considered by most people as being intolerant and offensive. "Who is God to say that 'free sex' is wrong?" And what about same-sex marriage? The Supreme Court decision on this issue is a travesty. It should never have to come before any court. Yet two of the Supreme Court justices have performed same sex marriages! Do they believe our report?

Christians in the United States are being branded as intolerant, homophobes and worse. Some are losing their businesses because of their stand for righteousness. Who believes our report?

Christian leaders in many countries are now being replaced by Muslim leaders who promise to "clean things up". Do they believe our report? In every case the report is not believed and the leaders reject anything to do with the One True God.

In John 12:37-41 we read, "But though he had done so many miracles before them, yet they believed not on him: That the saying of Esaias the prophet might be fulfilled, which he spake, **'Lord, who hath believed our report? and to whom hath the arm of the Lord been revealed?'** Therefore they could not believe, because that Esaias said again 'He hath blinded their eyes, and hardened their heart; that they should not see with their eyes, nor understand with their heard, and be converted, and I should heal them.' These things said Esaias, when he saw his glory, and spake of him." Note that v. 41 almost word for word repeats what was said in Is. 6:9-10.

The Apostle Paul writes in Romans 10:1-16, "1Brethren, my heart's desire and prayer to God for Israel is that they might be saved. 2For I bear them record that they have a zeal of God, but not according to knowledge. 3For they being ignorant of God's righteousness, and going about to establish their own righteousness, have not submitted themselves unto the righteousness of God. 4For Christ is the end of the law for righteousness to every one that believeth. 5For Moses describeth the righteousness which is of the law, that the man who doeth those things shall live by them. 6But the righteousness which is of faith speaketh on this wise, Say not in thine heart, Who shall ascend into heaven?(that is, to bring Christ down from above:) 7Or, who shall descend into the deep: (that is, to being up Christ again from the dead.) 8But what saith it? The word is nigh thee, even in thy mouth, and in thy heart: that is, the word of faith, which we preach; 9That if thou shalt confess with thy mouth the Lord Jesus, and shalt believe in thine heart that God hath raised him from the dead, thou shalt be saved. 10For with the heart man believeth unto righteousness; and with the mouth confession is made unto salvation. 11For the scripture saith, 'Whosoever shalt believe on him shall not be ashamed.' (Ps. 118:22) 12For there is no difference between Jew and Greek: for the same Lord over all is rich unto all that call upon him. 13For whosoever shall call upon the name of the Lord shall be saved. 14How then shall they call upon him who they have not believed? and how shall they believe in him of whom they have not heard? 15And how shall they hear without a preacher? And how shall they preach, except they be sent? as it is written, 'How beautiful are the feet of them that preach the gospel of peace, and bring glad tidings of good things!' (Is. 52:7) 16But they have not all obeyed the gospel. **For Esaias saith, 'Lord, who hath believed our report?'**"

"To whom is the arm of the Lord being revealed?"

Many times in history the Bible has been declared illegal. Even in "Christian" England the Bible was once declared illegal and everyone was told to bring their copies of the Bible to a specific place in London where they would be burned. The leaders didn't believe our report. Interestingly, that exact location is where the British and Foreign Bible Society now has their headquarters and more copies of the Bible are being printed in one hour than were burned in that great fire. **The arm or the Lord is being revealed.**

We receive reports daily of many in the persecuted areas of the world who are believing our report. They are turning to the Lord and opening their hearts to Him even though it may mean their death to do so. There are great revivals going on. Recently in Pakistan 27,000 people received the Lord on one day. ISIS leaders are accepting the Lord. Mega Voice, a company in Israel that produces electronic Bibles that look like cell phones,[2] can't meet the demand for their products. Their products are programmed in over 4,600 languages. These are being distributed throughout the Muslim countries and people are listening to God's Word while appearing to be talking on their cell phones! The arm of the Lord is being revealed in Pakistan, Syria, Iran and Iraq as-well-as in many other persecuted countries.

There are those in Israel who don't believe our report. There is even a very strong and active anti-missionary organization known as Yad L'achim (Hand for the Brothers). They want to kill the prophets. They once told me personally, "Get out of town or we will carry you out in a coffin". But we continue to minister there and the number of believers is growing. **The arm of the Lord is being revealed.**

I once knew nearly every believer in the country of Israel. Today there is an explosive growth there and I can't even name all of the places where there are Messianic congregations and churches. The arm of the Lord is being revealed.

Many people can't believe as their eyes are blinded as mentioned by Paul above. Even though the evidence is clear and is open to anyone who will simply seek, they don't see what is right in front of their eyes. Many people would rather believe and follow evil than good, hatred rather than love, war rather than peace.

In Romans 1:20-23 we read, "[20]For the invisible things of him from the creation of the world are clearly seen, being understood by the things that are made, even his eternal power and Godhead; so that they are without excuse: [21]Because that, when they knew God, they glorified him not as God, neither were thankful; but became vain in their imaginations and their foolish heart was darkened. [22]Professing themselves to be wise, they became fools, [23]and changed the glory of the uncorruptible God into an image made like to corruptible man, and to birds, and fourfooted beasts, and creeping things."

The corruption was so bad that God hid His glory and grace so that they could not see, hear or obey. That is a really scary thought.

---

[2] https://megavoice.com/

> **Isaiah 53:2**
> He shall grow up before him as a tender plant,
> and as a root out of a dry ground:
> He hath nor form or comeliness;
> and when we shall see him, there is no beauty that we should desire him.

Poetically, we have here both extended and completive parallels. The original thought is extended and then completed from a different perspective, which is also extended. The first thought is from God's perspective, while the second is from man's perspective.

God says: "He shall grow up before him as a tender plant, <u>and</u> as a root out of a dry ground." God sees the Messiah as a tender child or plant who is vulnerable in all His ways. He needs to be watered or nourished. He needs to be taken care of, trained, guided, taught, nurtured, etc. He is totally helpless on his own. He comes into a barren or dry world that is desperate for water. The dry ground is apparently fertile, but needs to be broken up, worked, fertilized, watered, etc.

This describes the spiritual condition of Israel, and yes, the whole world at the time of the birth of the Messiah. Jesus came into this world at a time when the Jewish people were spiritually desperate. They were under the rule of Roman dictators. Many were still in Babylon, modern day Iraq. The religious trusted their rabbis, but not God. They followed meaningless rituals thinking that they were serving God, but were basically serving themselves. They followed a long list of rules, rituals, and ceremonies that had long since lost their meaning. There was a lot of religion, but none of the relationship described in Scripture. They recited prayers that they were taught, but they didn't pray. The situation hasn't changed much to this day, especially among the Orthodox.

We see a lot of that today. People worldwide recite prayers that have been written in books. The Jewish people bow to stones at the Western Wall, reciting or reading prayers, psalms, etc. But there is no real connection to the Creator of the Universe, the One person who can actually answer prayer. Judaism today is empty, dry ground desperately in need of water, fertilizer, etc. But so is the rest of the world. Where is the love, the joy, the peace promised by God? Religions abound, but they fail to connect to the King of the Universe. People write myriads of books on meditation, self help, pilgrimages, etc. They say to face a certain direction when praying. Some say to wear black or white or some particular color of clothes or shave one's head. This is all nonsense. This is dry ground.

Now look at what men say in the same verse; "He hath no form or comeliness; and when we shall see him, there is no beauty that we should desire him."

The Messiah is not going to be some great charismatic figure, political giant or movie star. He won't stand out from the crowd. He will fit in with the crowd and will easily be able to "get lost" in it. Jesus actually did that once in Nazareth when the people tried to throw Him over a cliff.

Jesus did exactly this. He fit in with the crowd. He attended services in the local synagogue. He visited the Temple and discussed Scripture with the teachers. As a man He taught in the Temple along with many other rabbis. But he didn't go with the establishment on many issues. He pointed out that the empty rituals were, in fact, empty rituals. He demonstrated how those involved in religion for money were frauds.

For the most part people didn't flock to see him. There were two exceptions, the feeding of the 5,000 and later the feeding of the 4,000; but people wanted to follow Him for the wrong reasons. They wanted free food, not a relationship with the Creator of the Universe. They quickly forgot what He taught and sought what they could gain for themselves at His expense.

Do people desire Him today? Do they seek Him out? NO! Even in the United States, which was founded on God's Word. Even in many of our churches His teachings are being watered down, abandoned and even thrown out entirely. Our Supreme Court should never have to take a case to decide on the definition of marriage. Our churches should never have to defend themselves against society. Christian businesses should never have to decide to cater to anti-God groups or people. Today even some pastors are addicted to pornography, are liars, cheats, thieves and more. People pay a lot of money to see a movie star, rock star, etc. with no values; but not to seek and praise Jesus Christ, the Messiah. In many countries right now Christians are being murdered simply for identifying with Jesus.

Notice the promise given here. It says "**when** we shall see him" not **if** we shall see him. This is a definite promise, a positive statement. It will happen. God promised. It did happen physically when Jesus lived as a human being on this earth. The problem is that when people really did see Him they didn't recognize Him. He wasn't a movie star. He didn't stand out from the crowd.

How many people passed Jesus on the street and never knew who He was? Probably thousands. If He were to dress like we do and walk among us how many of us would recognize Him? If we heard about him would we seek Him? Put yourselves in the shoes of those who lived where He did when He did. What would be your response? Would you become a follower or disciple? Would you consider Him to be a crackpot, just another teacher or would you recognize Him as the Messiah? If you would have heard Him teach, what would have been your response? Would you have followed Him or would you have been among those mentioned in v. 3?

> **Isaiah 53:3**
> He is despised and rejected of men;
> a man of sorrows,
> acquainted with grief:
> And we hid as it were our faces from him;
> he was despised,
> and we esteemed him not.

Here we see the same pattern as in v. 2. First we have God's perspective and then man's perspective on the same theme—the rejection of the very One who came to bring peace, love and joy to all. Again, each perspective is extended, restating the previous thought in different words. Here the thought is extended twice, not just once as previously.

"He was despised and rejected of men". Throughout the Gospels we see that Jesus was, indeed, despised. The religious rulers hated Him as He constantly contradicted them—using Scripture. They were considered scholars and Jesus grew up in a small town where many of the people were illiterate. They sat under the great teachers and he sat under a local rabbi who couldn't get a better job. But He always had an answer as to why they were wrong. This infuriated them.

The situation hasn't changed much throughout the centuries that have followed. People have continuously been martyred for their faith from the time that Cain killed his brother, Abel. In Acts 6:9-15 we have the account of the murder of Stephen. Just as with Jesus, the accusers had to provide false testimony.

The book of Hebrews was written to the Jewish believers in Jerusalem who were under attack. The writer encouraged them to remain faithful to the Scriptures. The apostles were all murdered except John. Thomas was in his 90's when he was murdered in India, but he was still murdered for his faith.

Today Christians are being killed every day for the only crime being that they follow Jesus.

Homosexuals proudly parade their perversions in annual parades around the world. Explicit sexual behavior between men are the norm in many of these parades through the centers of cities. Sodom and Gomorrah were destroyed for lesser behavior.

I remember an allegorical magazine article in Reader's Digest many years ago where the leaders of the universe met together to discuss how to stop wars. They were all in great despair as they recounted the death, destruction, etc. on their planets. Then finally it was time for the representative from earth to speak. He reported, "The Prince of Peace came to our planet." They were all shocked and asked what happened. The representative from earth replied, "We killed Him." The others were shocked and asked why. He didn't know.

Jesus was a "man of sorrows". We never read in the Scriptures where Jesus laughed. We read that He wept, but nothing about Him laughing. Most people get upset when they are rejected. Look how any of us feel when someone makes fun of us or curses us out, etc. We definitely get upset. We should. But remember, these same people hate Jesus. That is worse. Often when we try to share Jesus, especially with Muslims or Jews they get upset and curse us. We are trying to rescue them from eternal hell, but they don't realize it. They don't see that they are in danger.

Jesus was also "acquainted with grief". He knew rejection, death, and sorrow. After all, He created the universe. He saw first hand Adam's sin. He witnessed the murder of Abel by Cain. He saw how people treated the prophets. As a baby He experienced the rejection and attempted murder by Herod. He was well ac-quainted with grief long before He was born in Bethlehem.

"We hid, as it were, our faces from him".

Psalm 53:1-6 reads: "**The fool hath said in his heart, *There is* no God.** Cor-rupt are they, and have done abominable iniquity: ***there is* none that doeth good**. 2God looked down from heaven upon the children of men, to see if there were any that did understand, that did seek God. 3**Every one of them is gone back: they are altogether become filthy; *there is* none that doeth good, no, not one**. 4Have the workers of iniquity no knowledge? who eat up my people as they eat bread: they have not called upon God. 5There were they in great fear, where no fear was: for God hath scattered the bones of him that encampeth against thee: thou hast put them to shame, because God hath despised them. 6Oh that the **salvation of Israel** were come out of Zion! When God bringeth back the captivity of his people, Jacob shall rejoice, and Israel shall be glad." (This text is also found in Ps. 14.)

"He was despised and we esteemed Him not."

People don't want to even consider the possibility that God exists. They want to do their own thing, whatever that means. Evil prevails on all sides. It is up to us as believers to shine the Light on the people around us. They need desperately what we have. But they don't want to admit it. People are not seeking Him. Jesus came, suffered and died for our sins. We need to share that news with those around us.

A Muslim to whom I was witnessing recently said, "There is heaven and the oven." He was right. But he is headed down the wrong path. He is not seeking the Lord. He is trying to follow Islam.

People despise Jesus and they don't care one bit. Some even admit that they are headed for hell. I have known people to even joke about it.

Jeremiah 17:9 states, "The heart *is* deceitful above *all things*, and desperately wicked: who can know it?"

Romans 3:23 states, "For *all have sinned*, and come short of the glory of God."

> **Isaiah 53:4-6**
> Surely he hath borne our griefs,
>   and carried our sorrows:
> yet we did esteem him stricken,
>   smitten of God,
>   and afflicted.
> But he was wounded for our transgressions,
>   he was bruised for our iniquities;
> The chastisement of our peace was upon him;
>   and with his stripes we are healed.
> All we like sheep have gone astray;
>   we have turned every one to his own way;
> and the LORD hath laid on him the iniquity of us all.

Here we see the crucifixion from the foot of the cross. We see the pain that the Messiah would suffer due to our sins. This is far more than a view of Jesus on the cross wearing a crown of thorns. Here we feel the emotions, sorrow, pain, grief and more because of our sins. We see the result and how our wrong actions have affected Jesus, the Son of God, the King of kings and Lord of lords. We hear the cries as the whip strikes His body, feel the emotions as the false accusations fly and jerk in pain as His beard is pulled out, the crown of thorns is placed on His head and the nails are driven into His hands and feet. Then He is raised up naked before the crowd of witnesses for all to see.

Only a few believers showed up at the crucifixion of Jesus. Among them was Mary, His mother; John the Apostle and a few others. Peter, the faithful servant was absent—sunk in his own grief for having betrayed Him, not once, but three times—when Jesus needed support the most. Among the unbelievers present two repent and open their hearts to Him. One is a thief who deserved to die. The other is the centurion who headed up the detail that day. To some of the onlookers this is just another crucifixion, one of many as they were so common that few people paid any attention.

Notice the progression from one verse to the next. In v. 4 we see that He bore **our** griefs and carried our sorrows, but we didn't pay any attention. This is the situation of the common person. Jesus died for all, but very few pay any attention. Most don't even notice—even if they are told. To them Jesus is just another famous religious teacher in history. They don't "get it". They don't understand. Neither do they care. Some say, "He isn't for me." Others say, "He is for the Christians, but not us." Most Jewish people simply answer, "Jesus isn't for the Jews."

But Isaiah was a Jewish prophet and the personal pronouns include all Jews. They include all people, but especially Jews. But the people hated Isaiah and his message. They eventually murdered him in order to get him to be quiet. Isaiah wouldn't give up. He preached every day—**every** day. He pleaded with the people to follow the Lord, but they refused to listen. He did everything he could to get their attention including sometimes preaching while naked. To the people Isaiah was a crazy man. It is good that there weren't any psychiatrists back then, but the people still wouldn't listen. (Isaiah 20:1-4)

We see the same situation today. I don't know of any preachers who get people's attention by going naked. But, today, such people would be put in prison. Isaiah was desperate to get the message across. But, no matter what he did, the people still refused to heed his warnings or listen to his message.

Isaiah knew what was coming. True, this was 700 years before the Messiah came into this world, but the message was still the same: get the peoples' attention and convince them that they need a Savior.

Jesus often healed the sick. In Matt. 8:16-17 we have a situation that specifically quotes Is. 53:4. It reads, "When the even was come, they brought unto him many that were possessed with devils: and he cast out the spirits with his word, and healed all that were sick: that it might be fulfilled which was spoken by Esaias the prophet, saying, "Himself took our infirmities, and bare our sicknesses."

Jesus continues to heal today. A close friend of ours, who is a Muslim, was healed from bleeding 4 months after she gave birth to her daughter after we anointed her with oil and prayed for her. Then a several months later she was still having terrible back pain since giving birth. We again anointed her and prayed for her and her daughter, who wasn't doing very well. Both have been healed. Our friend no longer has back pain and her daughter is now healthy and growing.

> **Isaiah 53:5**
> But he was wounded for our transgressions,
> he was bruised for our iniquities;
> The chastisement of our peace was upon him;
> and with his stripes we are healed.

This is partially quoted by Paul in Rom. 4:25 where we read, "...who was delivered for our offences, and was raised again for our justification." This refers to both vv. 5 and 6. Paul again refers to this passage in his wonderful declaration of the Gospel in I Corinthians 15:3-4 where it states, "For I delivered unto you first of all that which I also received, how that Christ died for our sins according to the scriptures; and that he was buried, and that he rose again the third day according to the scriptures." Here Paul referred to Is. 53, especially v. 5.

Paul and the Gospel writers were all very familiar with Isaiah 53. They referred to it or quoted it often in their speaking and writings.

The Messiah willingly endured being ridiculed, beaten, tortured, flogged and eventually crucified so that we might be forgiven of our sins. We see back in Is. 52:14 that due to this torture he was "marred more than any other man". Very few, if any, of the paintings or drawings of the crucifixion even come close to the horror that Jesus endured. The movies sure don't. His flesh was torn off exposing torn and scraped muscles. His blood was all over the place. It would have splattered all over his torturers, the stones would have been slippery with it. How He could walk at all after all that, let alone carry something as heavy as a cross, is beyond human imagination. I imagine that the crew who had to clean up the mess in front of the Citadel where the flogging took place would have been sick to their stomachs. It is incomprehensible.

> **Isaiah 53:6**
> All we like sheep have gone astray;
>   we have turned every one to his own way;
>   and the LORD hath laid on him the iniquity of us all.

This verse is extremely important and should be memorized by every believer. Every one of us has sinned. There are no exceptions. We have all gone astray.

Referring to believers as sheep is not a compliment in the Bible, though we are often called that. Jesus referred to Himself as the good shepherd. He often talked about believers as His "sheep". Sheep have a tendency to do their own thing. They wander a LOT. That is why shepherds have dogs who are trained to bring the sheep back to the flock. Sheep rarely, if ever, pay attention for more than a few seconds. They are always following their noses and do not pay attention. Sound like anyone you know? Sheep think that they know what is right. Their opinion is the most important no matter what the shepherd thinks or wants. His rules don't matter. They see greener grass somewhere else. Sound familiar?

I remember as a young boy once seeing a lone sheep by the side of the road. We lived in the Mojave Desert in California and were on our way home from a trip somewhere, probably visiting my grandparents. The shepherd and flock had moved on. I wanted my father to stop so we could rescue that lost sheep. The shepherd and rest of the flock were nowhere in sight. The sun was bright and the day was growing hotter by the minute. There was no water around. The water source had moved on with the shepherd and his water wagon. That lost sheep was prey to anything that would come by. It could easily wander out onto the highway and be killed. Or it could be attacked by a hyena or other predator that roamed the desert looking for food. But my father told me that that sheep would run from us as it wouldn't recognize our voices. We weren't the shepherd. Sheep only respond positively to their own shepherd's voice.

Jesus talks about this in John 10:22-28: "And it was at Jerusalem the feast of the dedication (Hanukah), and it was winter. And Jesus walked in the temple in Solomon's porch. Then came the Jews round about him, and said unto him, How long dost thou make us to doubt? If thou be the Christ (Messiah), tell us plainly. Jesus answered them, I told you, and ye believed me not: the works that I do in my Father's name, they bear witness of me. But ye believe not (Is. 53:1-3), because ye are not of my sheep, as I said unto you. My sheep hear my voice, and I know them, and they follow me (Is. 53:8): And I give unto them eternal life; and they shall never perish, neither shall any man pluck them out of my hand (Is. 53:10b)." We see Is. 53:1 referred to in v. 25. They were told, but didn't believe.

In Isaiah 59:2 it states, "But your iniquities have separated between you and your God." In I Kings 8:46a and II Chron. 6:36a we read, "For there is no man that sinneth not". Wow! That isn't politically correct! It is all-inclusive. It states that everyone who ever lived up to that time had sinned. Then Ezekiel takes this further in Ezekiel 18:4 where he states, "The soul that sinneth, it shall die!" Oy vey! What to do? We need Messiah NOW!

Because we sinned, God loved us so much that He was willing to send His only Son to die for us to make atonement for our sins. The sacrifices of the Tenach (Old Testament) only covered the sins. The term Yom Kippur means "day of covering". Sins in the Old Testament (Tenach) were only covered. They weren't taken away, forgiven or forgotten. It was only the sacrifice of Jesus that provided that. The Lord has laid on Him ALL of our sins. In I John 1:9 we read, "If we confess our sins, he is faithful and just to *forgive* us our sins, and to *cleanse* us from ALL unrighteousness."

Then John continues in the next verse, "If we say that we have not sinned, we make him a liar, and his word is not in us." That is extremely important. We have all sinned. If we say that we haven't, we make Jesus a liar. We make the prophets to be liars. We make God to be a liar. But there are many people today who claim just that. Anyone who states, "I have never sinned" just did. "**ALL** we, like sheep have gone astray." In the New Testament the Apostle Paul wrote in Rom. 3:23, "For all have sinned, and come short of the glory of God." And in I John 1:8-10 we have a fantastic sandwich. In v. 8 we read, "If we say that we have no sin, we deceive ourselves, and the truth is not in us." In v. 10 we read again, "If we say that we have not sinned, we make him (Jesus) a liar, and his word is not in us." But there is a wonderful piece of meat in this bitter sandwich. In v. 9 we read, "**If we confess our sins, he is faithful and just to forgive us our sins, and to cleanse us from all unrighteousness.**"

In the last part of Isaiah 53:6 we read the first of six recurring statements, "and the LORD hath laid on him the iniquity of us all". This theme is repeated in v. 8 where is states, "for the transgression of my people was he stricken" and in v. 10 where we read, "thou shalt make his soul and offering for sin" and again v. 11 where it is written, "he shall bear their iniquities" and finally in v. 12 we see the two final statements where it says "he bare the sin of many, and made intercession for the transgressors."

> **Isaiah 53:7**
> He was oppressed,
>   and he was afflicted,
>   yet he openeth not his mouth:
> he is brought as a lamb to the slaughter,
>   and as a sheep before her shearers is dumb,
>   so he openeth not his mouth.

This verse is the focal point of this chapter and the central theme of Isaiah 40:1-66:24. It is also the exact center of this long Messianic poem as well as Isaiah 53.

Everything in this long Messianic poem preceding this verse and everything following it points to the statement "he was brought as a lamb to the slaughter". When Jesus appeared at the location where John was baptizing people, John saw Him and cried out, "**Behold, the Lamb of God, which taketh away the sins of the world.**" (Jn. 1:29) This is a direct reference to Is. 53:7. That one statement summarizes the whole of Isaiah 53 and pinpoints the central theme of the Bible. <u>**Jesus is the Lamb.**</u> He is the Lamb of God. And He died for the sins of the world. Yet, at His trial Pilate was perplexed as Jesus entered no defense. Others also tried to get Him to defend Himself. But He remained silent.

This verse is fulfilled in all four gospels and in the book of Acts.

Note:

- **Matthew 26:62-63** "And the high priest arose, and said unto him, **Answerest thou nothing?** what is it which these witness against thee? But Jesus held his peace. And the high priest answered and said unto him, I adjure thee by the living God, that thou tell us whether thou be the Christ (Messiah), the Son of God."

- **Mark 15:3-5** "And the chief priests accused him of many things: but he answered nothing. And Pilate asked him again, saying, **Answerest thou nothing?** behold how many things they witness against thee. But Jesus yet answered nothing; so that Pilate marveled."

- **Luke 23:8-9** "And when Herod saw Jesus, he was exceeding glad: for he was desirous to see him of a long season, because he had heard many things of him; and he hoped to have seen some miracle done by him. Then he questioned with him in many words; but **he answered him nothing.**"

- **John 19:8-9** "When Pilate therefore heard that saying, he was the more afraid; And went again into the judgment hall, and saith unto Jesus, Whence art thou? But **Jesus gave him no answer**."

- **This is quoted in Acts 8:32-33** "The place of the scripture which he read was this, He was led as a sheep to the slaughter; and like a lamb dumb before his shearer, **so opened he not his mouth**: In his humiliation his judgment was taken away: and who shall declare his generation? (Is. 53:8) for his life is taken from the earth."

Peter also referred to this verse in **I Peter 2:23-25**. But for the context we need to begin in v. 18 and then note especially in 21-25.

> "18Servants, be subject to your masters with all fear: not only to the good and gentle, but also to the froward. 19For this is thankworthy if a man for conscience toward God endure grief, suffering wrongfully. 20For what glory is it, if, when ye be buffeted for your faults, ye shall take it patiently? but if, when ye do well, and suffer for it, ye take it patiently, this is acceptable with God. 21For even hereunto were ye called: because Christ also suffered for us, leaving us an example, that ye should follow his steps: 22Who did no sin neither was guile found in his mouth: 23Who, when he was reviled, reviled not again; when he suffered, he threatened not; but committed himself to him that judgeth righteously: 24Who his own self bare our sins in his own body on the tree, that we, being dead to sins, should live unto righteousness: by whose stripes ye were healed. 25For ye were as sheep going astray; but are now returned unto the Shepherd and Bishop of your souls."

In the first part of this Peter tells servants (or in today's society, employees) to be good workers, even if your boss is bad. Then he uses the example of Jesus being so obedient to the Father that He was willing to suffer persecution for us so that we would receive forgiveness of sin. Jesus didn't grumble or complain. He followed His "boss" to the end. How much would any of us complain? We complain in far less situations than this.

Paul shares the same idea in Philippians 2:1-11 where we read, "1If there be therefore any consolation in Christ, if any comfort of love, if any fellowship of the Spirit, if any bowels and mercies, 2Fulfill ye my joy, that ye be likeminded, having the same love, being of one accord, of one mind. 3Let nothing be done through strife or vainglory; but in lowliness of mind let each esteem other better than themselves. 4Look not every man on his own things, but every man also on the things of others. 5Let this mind be in you, which was also in Christ Jesus: 6Who, being in the form of God, thought it not robbery to be equal with God: 7But made himself of no reputation, and took upon him the form of a servant, and was made in the likeness of men: 8And being found in fashion as a man, he humbled himself, and became obedient unto death, even the death of the cross. 9Wherefore God also hath highly exalted him, and given him a name which is above every name: 10That at the name of Jesus every knee should bow, of things in heaven, and things in earth, and things under the earth; 11And that every tongue should confess that Jesus Christ is Lord, to the glory of God the Father." Jesus was "obedient unto death, even the death of the cross." As a result, His reward was far greater than if He hadn't followed through with the plan of redemption. Now everyone must confess that Jesus is Lord, either in this life or in hell. Satan knows and has to confess that Jesus is Lord. We must also. It is far better to be obedient here in this life and to receive our reward in heaven than to deny Him now and have to recognize who He is in hell when it is too late.

Jesus, the Messiah, the Son of God took upon Himself the role of a servant. At any time He could have used His authority to destroy His persecutors. He could have brought fire down on the Pharisees and Sadducees, those who persecuted Him, Pontius Pilate, those who drove the nails into His hands and feet, etc. He could have destroyed them all. But He chose to suffer ridicule, pain and even death so that He might be the ultimate example for us.

Those who ridicule Him today will, sooner or later, have to recognize Who He is, the King of Kings, Lord of Lords, Almighty God, Jehovah.

Jesus is patient—far more than any of us. None of us would suffer as He did. We especially wouldn't do it silently. Then on the cross for Him to cry out, "Father, forgive them, for they know not what they do" is the ultimate example of how to be a good servant. We easily become angry at little things. Jesus didn't display His anger at the cross. It will be expressed in the future, and especially in eternity. His patience is about to run out. But there is still time to repent and accept His sacrifice for our sins.

> **Isaiah 53:8**
> He was taken from prison and from judgment:
>   and who shall declare his generation?
> for he was cut off out of the land of the living:
>   for the transgression of my people was he stricken.

Now we begin the part where God's perspective is emphasized. We no longer see the pronouns "us", "we", etc. These have been replaced by "He", "his" and "my". "My" is God speaking. "My people" refers to the Jewish people. Jesus was the Jewish Messiah.

There are two concepts of Messiah. The first is Messiah ben Joseph, which refers to the suffering Messiah. The second is Messiah ben David, which is the reigning Messiah or Messiah the King. Jewish thinking is that there are two Messiahs, one who suffers and dies and one who conquers and subdues His enemies and reigns over the earth. They don't see the two as being the same person, but coming at two different times. Most rabbis today see only a reigning Messiah, one who will subdue and conquer all of Israel's enemies, eradicate anti-Semitism, evil and sin and who will usher in the Messianic Kingdom complete with a new Temple in Jerusalem.

This is, indeed, the position of the Temple Institute in Jerusalem which is an organization dedicated to building the third Temple. They have rebuilt the Menorah, altar of sacrifice, utensils for service, etc. for the Temple. The stones are carved and waiting to be placed on the Temple Mount. They are training priests and know who the high priest will be. All is in place ready to go.

Let us take the first question, skip the second one (for now) and go to the third statement: "He was taken from prison and from judgment...for he was cut off out of the land of the living." At some point Jesus was probably kept in a holding cell with another prisoner, a criminal, with the same name. But in the New Testament he is called Barabbas. This is fulfilled in Matt. 27:15-26, Mark 15:6-15 and Luke 23:13-25. His real name was Yeshua bar Abba or Jesus son of the Father. Jesus was the true Yeshua bar Abba. He was not the son of Joseph, so He couldn't be called Yeshua bar Yosef. The term "bar Abba" means "son of the Father". So, there is the true Son of God Who was the Messiah, the Righteous One and there was the fake son of God, who was a criminal and was in prison for taking part in an insurrection and for murder.

Pilate tried several times to get the people to release Jesus, but every time they cried out, concerning Jesus, "Crucify Him, Crucify Him". Since the Roman government had a practice of releasing a Jewish prisoner during Passover, Pilate offered them the choice of a criminal that they should have hated even more than Jesus Christ. They kept growing louder and louder saying concerning Jesus, the true Son of God, "Crucify Him, crucify Him." And concerning Barabbas, they chose to have him released.

This is in exact fulfillment of Is. 53:8a, c and d.

But now the question in the second part of 8b is interesting: "who shall declare his generation?" It would be necessary for someone or some people to tell others about what would take place. Of the thousands of crucifixions that took place, there would need to be messengers to tell why this one was different, why this one mattered. This is where the apostles, later believers and we come in. Yes, God is talking about us. We are to "go into all the world and preach the gospel" (Matt. 28:18-20, Mark 16:15). We have been commissioned to share the gospel, to tell others, and to bring them to Jesus, the Jewish Messiah.

The early believers began to share the Gospel. We see in Acts 2 the events at Pentecost. First, the people were gathered in an upper room and the Holy Spirit appeared in the form of a wind and flames above the people's heads. But they soon moved outside into a much larger area where many people heard the Gospel message in their own languages. Peter then began to preach and tell the people about Jesus, His life, death and resurrection.

In v. 38 he told them to repent and to be baptized. This verse has been misinterpreted by many people so that they think that salvation is by baptism. This is not true. Baptism doesn't save anyone. It is a sign of obedience. The structure of the Greek grammar here is a direct command for everyone to repent. It is an open invitation. Then the command to be baptized is a different form, which means to be identified with the death, burial and resurrection of Jesus. In I Cor. 10:2 the same phrase is used concerning identification with Moses.

The Jewish custom was for an individual to be baptized by the rabbi under whom he studied, thus identifying with that particular rabbi. Jesus was unusual as he did not baptize anyone, but commanded those who did repent to be baptized in His name.

In Acts 2:41 we see that approximately 3,000 people repented and were baptized on that day. A short time later in Acts 4:4 we see that 5,000 more were added.

In Acts 4:12 Peter was speaking to the Jewish leaders and he told them plainly, "Neither is there salvation in any other: for there is none other name under heaven, given among men, whereby we must be saved."

The movement continued to grow. Then in Acts 6 the Church begins to become organized and chose church officers, etc. In Acts 7 one of them, Stephen, was arrested and eventually stoned to death illegally by a Jewish mob. One of those who watched the clothes of those throwing the rocks was a young man named Saul. He later saw a vision of Jesus in Acts 9 and eventually became the great missionary, Paul.

With Paul the great missionary movement in what is now Turkey and Greece began. Thousands of people were saved. Churches were planted. The New Testament was written. The Gospel was then passed down from generation to generation to eventually reach us.

We are most familiar with Turkey and Europe, but the Gospel penetrated other areas as well. The Apostle Thomas went to India and planted churches along the way. He was murdered when he was 95 years old. There are churches in Iran and Iraq that date from the first century. In the summer of 2015 a church in Iraq was bombed that even had manuscripts from the first century, which were destroyed by the Muslims.

Others went to Africa, especially Ethiopia, North Africa and Egypt.

So, the question posed in Is. 53:8, "Who will declare His generation?" is answered quickly with "We will" or longer by many testimonies of over 2,000 years of lives being changed. That is continuing on today.

In the last phrase of verse 8 we see what would happen to Jesus and why. First, the Messiah would be killed. Then we see that it was for "the transgression of my people". This is God speaking. The Messiah would die for the Jewish people. Here we aren't told how He would die, just that it would happen. Earlier in Is. 52:13 we see that He would die by crucifixion.

Throughout the Old Testament the Jewish people are referred to again and again as "my people". But let us look at only one of those references, Is. 52:5-6. There we read, "Now therefore, what have I here, saith the LORD, that *my people* is taken away for naught? they that rule over them make them to howl, saith the LORD; and my name continually every day is blasphemed. Therefore *my people* shall know my name: therefore they shall know in that day that I am he that doth speak: behold, it is I."

Throughout the Gospels we see that Jesus went to the Jewish people. He called them "the lost sheep of the house of Israel" in Matt. 10:6 and 15:24. Indeed, they are also called by the same term in Ps. 119:176, where we read, "I have gone astray like a lost sheep; seek thy servant; for I do not forget thy commandments." This also brings us back to Is. 53:6a, "All we, like sheep, have gone astray..." Then in Jeremiah 50:6-7 we see, "My people hath been lost sheep: their shepherds have caused them to go astray, they have turned them away on the mountains: they have gone from mountain to hill, they have forgotten their resting place. All that found them have devoured them: and their adversaries said, We offend not, because they have sinned against the LORD, the habitation of justice, even the LORD, the hope of their fathers."

In Matthew 10:1-4 Jesus calls His disciples. In vv. 5-42 He commissions them for ministry. In verses 5 & 6 He tells them, "Go not into the way of the Gentiles, and into any city of the Samaritans enter ye not: but go rather to the lost sheep of the house of Israel."

In Matt. 15:21-28 Jesus has an encounter with a Gentile woman who wants Him to deliver her daughter from demons. But Jesus tested her and told her to go away. But she insisted. He told her in v. 24, "I am not sent but unto the lost sheep of the house of Israel." The woman persisted and was healed. Her faith became strong. This is one of the few cases where Jesus took care of a Gentile. There are others, such as the Centurion's daughter, the feeding of the 4,000 and others. But, mainly He stayed among His own people. He preached in synagogues, visited Jewish towns and spent time in the Temple in Jerusalem.

In John 1:11-13 we read, "He came unto his own, and his own received him not. But as many as received him, to them gave he power to become the sons of God, even to them that believe on his name: which were born, not of blood, nor of the will of the flesh, nor of the will of man, but of God."

What a sad commentary! God sent Moses, rescued them from 490 years of slavery, provided them with food, water and all that they needed. They didn't have to work for 40 years. He gave them the Torah so they would know how to live and treat each other and how to serve God. But they refused to obey. He sent prophets to warn and guide them, but they killed the messengers. Finally, He sent His Son to show His love and care. But He was killed too. What a sad commentary.

We see the same thing happening now. Those who stand for the Truth, for God's Word, and who try to bring people back to God are laughed at, beaten, put in prison and even killed. Solomon said in Eccl. 1:9, "...there is no new thing under the sun."

> **Isaiah 53:9**
> And he made his grave with the wicked,
> and with the rich in his death;
> because he had done no violence,
> neither was any deceit in his mouth.

Here we have three statements. The first refers to the crucifixion where Jesus was crucified between two thieves. (Luke 23:33-43) They were wicked. They deserved to die. One of them even admitted it, but pleaded with Jesus for forgiveness. The other refused. The one who repented was told "today you will be with me in paradise" (v. 43).

29

The second statement refers to Jesus' burial. He was buried in the tomb of Joseph of Arimathea, who was very wealthy. In fact, he and Nicodemus were two of the three most wealthy men in Jerusalem. I don't know who the third one was. Both of these men provided for Jesus' burial. Nicodemus provided the spices and burial cloths for wrapping His body. (Matt. 27:57-60, Mark 15:42-46, Luke 23:50-54 and John 19:31-42)

The third statement tells us that Jesus was innocent of all accusations, that He committed no crimes, not even any deception. This is seen in the testimony of the centurion in charge of the crucifixion. See Matt. 27:54, Mark 15:39-45 and Luke 23:47. The centurion realized that Jesus was not only innocent of all charges, but was truly the Messiah, the Son of God.

Isaiah 53:10-12
The Victory paragraph – Verse 10
Yet it pleased the LORD to bruise him;
    he hath put him to grief:
when thou shalt make his soul an offering for sin,
    he shall see his seed,
        he shall prolong his days,
            and the pleasure of LORD shall prosper in his hand.

On the surface, this is a VERY confusing verse. How is it possible that the LORD could possibly take pleasure from the grief, pain and suffering of the crucifixion of Jesus? Isn't that a bit like a terrorist or masochist? Why would Jehovah take pleasure in the suffering and death of His Son? The description of crucifixion from both the Scriptures and from reality cause most people to cringe, not rejoice. The pictures we see of crucifixions by ISIS of Christians in Syria are difficult to look at. Yet, here we are told that the LORD took pleasure in just such a scene. The pain and agony that Jesus went through is more than any other man.

Paul speaks about this in II Cor. 5:21. But we need to begin at verse 11 and read through the rest of the chapter.

> "[11]Knowing therefore the terror of the Lord, we persuade men; but we are made manifest unto God; and I trust also are made manifest in your consciences. [12]For we commend not ourselves again unto you, but give you occasion to glory on our behalf, that ye may have somewhat to answer them which glory in appearance, and not in heart. [13]For whether we be beside ourselves, it is to God: or whether we be sober, it is for your cause. [14]For the love of Christ constraineth us; because we thus judge, that if one died for all, then were all dead: [15]and that he died for all, that they which live should not henceforth

live unto themselves, but unto him which died for them, and rose again. [16]Wherefore henceforth know we no man after the flesh: yea, though we have known Christ after their flesh, yet now henceforth know we him no more. [17]***Therefore if any man be in Christ he is a new creature: old things are passed away: behold, all things are become new.*** [18]And all things are of God, who hath **reconciled** us to himself by Jesus Christ, and hath given to us the ministry of **reconciliation**; [19]to wit, that God was in Christ, **reconciling** the world unto himself, not imputing their trespasses unto them; and hath committed unto us the word of **reconciliation**. [20]Now then we are ambassadors for Christ, as thought God did beseech you by us; we pray you in Christ's stead, be ye **reconciled** to God. [21]***For he hath made him to be sin for us, who knew no sin; that we might be made the righteousness of God in him.***"

The result of Jesus' suffering and sacrifice for us allows us to become "new creations" (v. 17) and to be reconciled to the Father (vv. 18-20). We become new creations. Our old lives and sins are forgiven and washed away.

In Psalm 103:12 we read, "As far as the east is from the west, *so* far hath he removed our transgressions from us." Our sins are not simply covered over. They are removed. It is interesting that David didn't say "as far as the north is from the south...", but "as far as the east is from the west." If you go either north or south far enough you will end up going back the other direction once you reach the north or south pole. But you can travel either east or west and keep going in the same direction for all eternity and never go the other way, even though you will pass the starting point many times. It says, "he removed our transgressions from us." The key word here is "removed". They are taken away.

With the sacrifices of the Old Testament sins were simply covered, not removed. The term "Yom Kippur" means "Day of Covering". Back in Gen. 17 we have rules concerning blood. Blood is sacred. Without it there is no life. Jesus shed His blood on the cross. In Lev. 17:11 we read, "For the life of the flesh is in the blood: and I have given it to you upon the altar to make an atonement for your souls: for it is the blood that maketh an atonement for the soul." Here the word "atonement" is "kapar" in Hebrew, which means covering. In Hebrews 9:11-22 the writer speaks about the importance of the blood of Christ.

"[11]But Christ being come a high priest of good things to come, by a greater and more perfect tabernacle, not made with hands, that is to say, not of this building; [12]Neither by blood of goats and calves, but by his own blood he entered in once into the holy place, having obtained eternal redemption for us. [13]For the blood of bulls and of

31

goats, and the ashes of a heifer sprinkling the unclean, sanctifieth to the purifying of the flesh: 14How much more shall the blood of Christ who through the eternal Spirit offered himself without spot to God, purge your conscience from dead works to serve the living God? 15And for this cause he is the mediator of the new testament, that by means of death, for the redemption of the transgressions that were under the first testament, they which are called might receive the promise of eternal inheritance. 16For where a testament is, there must also of necessity be the death of the testator. 17For a testament is of force after men are dead: otherwise it is of no strength at all while the testator liveth. 18Whereupon neither the first testament was dedicated without blood. 19For when Moses had spoken every precept to all the people according to the law, he took the blood of calves and of goats, with water, and scarlet wool, and hyssop, and sprinkled both the book, and all the people, 20Saying, This is the blood of the testament which God hath enjoined unto you. 21Moreover he sprinkled with blood both the tabernacle, and all the vessels of the ministry. 22And almost all things are by the law purged with blood; and without the shedding of blood is no remission."

The blood of animals was used to sanctify, or make holy, certain artifacts or places. The blood of sacrificed animals was important. Each animal died in the process. None of them ever rose from the dead. They were killed, the blood drained and the animal then burned on the altar. This would have been a terrible thing to witness day-after-day for your entire life. The job of being a priest was not one that I would like to have. Finally, in v. 22 the writer quotes from Lev. 17:11, "without shedding of blood is no remission." The blood of bulls and goats only covered sins. It never erased sins. Yes, they were removed, but never erased. **The blood of Jesus erases our sins.**

Back to II Cor. 5:21. Here we read, "For he hath made him to be sin for us, who knew no sin; that we might be made the righteousness of God in him." Jesus, who had not committed even one single sin, became sin for us that we might become righteous, be reconciled to the Father, and be perfect in God's eyes, allowing us to enter His perfect Kingdom of Heaven for all eternity. WOW! HALLELUJAH!

Now let us return to Is. 53:10. Here we see that Jesus not only died for our sins, but rose victoriously. In the second half of the verse we have the resurrection. "...he shall see is seed". A dead person can't see anything. But in this description of the atonement, we are told that following His death, the Messiah would "see his seed". He will see those who follow Him.

In I Corinthians 15:12-20 we read,

"¹²Now if Christ be preached that he rose from the dead, how say some among you that there is no resurrection of the dead? ¹³But if there be no resurrection of the dead, then is Christ not risen: ¹⁴And **if Christ be not risen, then is our preaching in vain, and your faith is also vain**. ¹⁵Yea, and we are found false witnesses of God; because we have testified of God that he raised up Christ: whom he raised not up, if so be that the dead rise not. ¹⁶**For if the dead rise not, then is not Christ raised: ¹⁷And if Christ be not raised, your faith is vain; ye are yet in your sins**. ¹⁸Then they also which are fallen asleep in Christ are perished ¹⁹*If in this life only we have hope in Christ, we are of all men most miserable*. ²⁰But now is Christ risen from the dead, and become the firstfruits of them that slept."

Next we read in Isaiah 53:10, "he shall prolong his days". How can one's days be prolonged once he is dead? It can happen only if the dead has been raised back to life.

In John 11:1-46 Jesus raised Lazarus from the dead. The Jewish leaders taught that it might be possible to raise someone from the dead for up to 3 days as one's soul hovered above the body for that long. But it would not be possible to raise someone from the dead after that. Lazarus was raised from the dead after four days, something that was taught that even Messiah wouldn't be able to do. Jesus prolonged the days of Lazarus.

Once while ministering in Israel we were introduced to a man named Semyon who shared how that five years before we met him he had died of cancer. His body was taken to the morgue in Tel Ha Shomer Hospital in Haifa and made ready for an autopsy the next morning. During the night, while laying on the table for the autopsy, Semyon's body was touched and he awoke. He heard a voice telling him, "You will not die, but shall live." He scared a few nurses and doctors who later examined him. They discovered that there was no sign that he had ever had cancer and was in perfect health. Semyon lived many more years before he passed away of natural causes. His life was prolonged.

But the passage tells us that the Messiah's life would be prolonged. Jesus died on the cross, was buried in a tomb and remained there for 3 days. But He didn't stay there. On the third day He rose from the dead, never to die again. Both Lazarus and our friend Semyon did die again. But Jesus rose 40 days later into heaven while His disciples watched. (Matthew 28, Mark 16, Luke 24, John 20, I Corinthians 15.

The last phrase reads, "and the pleasure of the LORD shall prosper in his hand." Here we see the word "pleasure" repeated for the second time in this verse, but in a totally different context from the first phrase. Here there is rejoicing. The Church is growing. People are getting saved. They are becoming new creatures. They are being reconciled to Him. This leads us to vv. 11 & 12 where we see victory out of tragedy.

> **Isaiah 53:11**
> He shall see of the travail of his soul,
>   and shall be satisfied:
> by his knowledge shall my righteous servant justify many;
>   for he shall bear their iniquities.

Let us look at Psalm 16:10-11 where we read:

"For thou wilt not leave my soul in hell (sheol);
      neither wilt thou suffer thine Holy One to see corruption.
Thou wilt shew me the path of life:
      in thy presence is fulness of joy;
            at thy right hand there are pleasures for evermore."

The Messiah would die, but would not see corruption. His body would not decay. He would rise from the dead before that would happen. David looked forward to a risen Messiah who would remove all of his sins.

In this psalm David looks forward to eternal life with God. In v. 1 he ask for the Lord to "preserve" him as he has put his trust in God (elohim). But 4 times (vv. 2, 5, 7 & 8) he identifies God as LORD or Jehovah.

In vv. 2 and 3 we read: "O my soul, thou has said unto my LORD (Yahweh): thou are my Lord (Adonai), my goodness extendeth not to thee; but to the saints that are in the earth, and to the excellent, in whom is all my delight." Wow! David isn't thinking so much of himself, but of the believers in the years to come. This applies directly to you and me. To all who have accepted the Lord. Numerous places in Scripture we are referred to as saints. Paul often began his letters addressing them to the saints in a particular place. Saints in Scripture are not people who have been dead for 300 years or so and then elevated to sainthood by some council. Saints, in Scripture are all believers. In both the Old Testament (Tenach) and New Testament saints refer to living people. When the Apostle Paul addressed letters "To the saints at..." he wasn't writing letters to dead people, but to those who were alive and living for the Lord. Anyone who has accepted Jesus as Savior is a saint according to Scripture.

In Psalm 16:5 David relies on the Lord for his eternal reward, his inheritance when he writes, "The LORD is the portion of mine inheritance and of my cup:

thou maintainest my lot." This is not an earthly inheritance from a relative who has died, but it is our inheritance in eternal life due to our accepting the gift of salvation from the Messiah and Savior who died and rose from the grave victoriously.

Look at Psalm 16:7. "I will bless the LORD, who hath given me counsel: my reins also instruct me in the night seasons." Here we see David blessing and thanking the Lord for instructing him not only during the day, but in his innermost being during the night. The New King James says "heart". In Hebrew the term is עצני, which literally means kidneys. In Russian it is внутренность, which means our innermost being. In the KJV it says "reins", the things that are used to control the direction of a horse. Basically, we are to be thanking the Lord for teaching us day and night. We can know that something is true, because we know it deeply inside us. In the book of I John we have the term "I know" used over and over again. The Greek term means "I know, because it is absolute fact." David knew with absolute certainty that his hope was eternal, that his salvation was secure. He didn't have any doubts at all. He faced eternity with joy.

Psalm 16:8 reads, "I have set the LORD always before me: because he is at my right hand, I shall not be moved." Because of the certainty of v. 7 David's faith was sure. No one, nothing would ever be able to persuade him otherwise. David made a lot of mistakes. He sinned a lot. He committed adultery and murder. Yet he knew that his salvation was sure. He knew, absolutely, where he would spend eternity.

In Psalm 16:9 David is ecstatic with joy looking forward to eternity with the Lord. "Therefore my heart is glad, and my glory rejoiceth: my flesh also shall rest in hope."

Vv. 10 and 11, which were quoted on the previous page at the introduction to this section, look forward to eternity. V. 10 is interesting. David looked forward to a bodily resurrection. Note his words, "For thou wilt not leave my soul in hell (sheol); neither wilt thou suffer thine Holy One to see corruption." This is interesting. David died. His body did suffer corruption. You can visit David's tomb in Jerusalem today. Jesus spoke about it when He was there. But this speaks of another "David" the Messiah. Turn to Acts 13:35-37. Here we read, "Wherefore he saith also in another psalm, Thou shalt not suffer thine Holy One to see corruption. For David, after he had served his own generation by the will of God, fell on sleep, and was laid unto his fathers, and saw corruption: But he, whom God raised again, saw no corruption." David's body did suffer corruption, but the body of "the Holy One", Jesus Christ did not see corruption.

Then the last verse of Ps. 16, v. 11, describes eternal life as the "path of life", "fullness of joy" and "pleasures for evermore". Life won't be dull there. We won't get bored. Some descriptions of heaven seem rather boring after awhile. But, believe me, we will never get bored. We won't get tired. We won't get sick. We will never become angry. No one will ever have to yell at us. No one will ever want to. That last word, "forevermore", is eternal. It has no end.

Now back to Is. 53:11. Just as with David in Ps. 16, the Lord will be pleased with us. He will overlook our sins and forgive them. He will be satisfied with us, just as He was with David. We read, "by his knowledge shall my righteous servant justify many; for he shall bear their iniquities." God knows everything. He knows our thoughts. He knows the things that we don't want anyone to know. Yet He saw fit to send Jesus to die for our sins—to justify us.

The entire chapter of Romans 5 deals with justification by faith. In v. 1 we read, "Therefore, being justified by faith, we have peace with God through our Lord Jesus Christ." This is the exact fulfillment of Is. 53:11. We have peace with God. We don't have to worry. We can relax in His arms. I could spend a long time on this chapter, but it merits an entire book of its own. Billy Graham once wrote a book on this chapter titled, "Peace With God". It has been translated into many languages. I remember giving a copy in Hebrew to a lady on the kibbutz where I worked in the summer of 1968. She treasured it greatly and read it over and over until she wore it out.

In Rom. 5:8 we read, "But God commendeth his love toward us, in that, while we were yet sinners, Christ died for us." Yes. Jesus did die for us. In v. 9 we see that "we are justified by his blood", just as is written in Is. 53:10-12. In v. 10 it states, "For if, when we were enemies, we were **reconciled** to God by the death of his Son, much more being **reconciled**, we shall be saved by his life." And in v. 11 we find, "And not only so, but we also joy in God through our Lord Jesus Christ, by whom we have now received the **atonement**." Jesus bore our iniquities as it states in Is. 53:11 and our sins as mentioned in v. 12.

> **Isaiah 53:12**
> Therefore will I divide him a portion with the great,
>   and he shall divide the spoil with the strong;
> Because he hath poured out his soul unto death:
>   and he was numbered with the transgressors;
> And he bare the sin of many,
>   and made intercession for he transgressors.

Here we have a three-part summary of the entire chapter. This is written about someone who is living and active. He died, but was resurrected. This is a statement of victory, a declaration of what is to come. The outlook is positive, exciting and glorious. First, we have a direct and very positive statement followed by the reasons for that victory. In I Cor. 15:26 we read, "The last enemy that shall be destroyed is death." Here in v. 12 we see the declaration of victory over death. You can't divide inheritances among dead people. The word "portion" in the first phrase and "spoil" in the second are synonyms for the same thing. They refer to the inheritance of the saints in eternity. The "great" and the "strong" are also synonymous. These are those who rise from the dead, the saints, who are described earlier in I Cor. 15 as mentioned earlier. These are the saints, those who have accepted the Messiah, whose sins are forgiven and wiped away.

Notice in the second portion of v. 12 that the Messiah died and was numbered with the transgressors—even though He had never sinned as mentioned earlier. He died between two thieves after being falsely accused and had been given the sentence that the false Bar Abba deserved, but was let go.

Finally, in the third statement in v. 12 we see that the Messiah made intercession for us—the transgressors. He bore our sins. He took our burdens, our sins, our diseases, our lies, our false statements, our crimes, our wrongdoings. He died for it all. Because of His sacrifice eternal life and joy is open to all. It is open to perverts, murderers, criminals of all types, liars, cheats, everyone.

Why would anyone ever want to reject what God has to offer through the Messiah as described in Isaiah 53? Why would anyone reject God's love? Why do people choose hell over heaven? I don't get it. What is your choice? If you have not done so yet, choose the Messiah. He paid it all.

We urge you to believe our report. Your future depends on it.

† † †